The BASIC STEPS *of* BIBLE STUDY

KAY ARTHUR
and DAVID ARTHUR *with* PETE DE LACY

HARVEST HOUSE PUBLISHERS
EUGENE, OREGON

Cover design by Bryce Williamson

Cover photo © PJ66431470 / iStock Photo

The Basic Steps of Bible Study
Taken from *How to Study Your Bible*
Published by Harvest House Publishers
Eugene, Oregon 97408
www.harvesthousepublishers.com

ISBN 978-0-7369-7979-5 (pbk.)
ISBN 978-0-7369-7980-1 (eBook)

Library of Congress Cataloging-in-Publication Data is on file at the Library of Congress, Washington, DC.

Printed in the United States of America

19 20 21 22 23 24 25 26 27 / BP-RD / 10 9 8 7 6 5 4 3 2 1

Contents

The Joy and Value of Inductive Study

The Bible was written so that anyone who wants to know who God is and how they are to live in a way that pleases Him can read it and find out.

God wants to bring us into intimacy with Himself. He wants to be a Father to us. In order to have that relationship, however, God has to talk to us. He wants to explain to us who He is and how we can be brought into a close, wonderful relationship with Him. He also wants us to understand the blessings of a life of obedience to His Word and the consequences of disobeying Him. And He wants us to know the truth about life and what is going to happen in the future.

The Bible tells us everything we need to know about life. That, my friend, is why you need to study it for yourself.

There are many ways to study the Bible, and there are many excellent study aids available to help you with specific books of the Bible. But the most important thing you need to remember is that to find out what the Bible says, you need to read it yourself in a way that will help you discover what it says, what it means, and how you are to apply it to your life. And the best way to do this is through the process called inductive study. Inductive study doesn't tell you what the Bible means or what you should believe. Instead, it teaches you a method of studying God's Word that can be applied to any portion of Scripture at any time for the rest of your life.

The main requirement in learning to study the Bible inductively is the willingness to slow down and really look at what the Scripture is saying. That may not sound too difficult, but in times like ours it is probably the most difficult part of the entire process. And to be honest, my friend, don't you sometimes wonder if our busyness—even for God—isn't often what's keeping us from being what God wants us to be?

Inductive Bible study uses the Bible itself as the primary source of information about the Bible. In inductive study you personally explore the Scriptures apart from conclusions Bible scholars and other people have drawn from their study of the Word. Though their labors are valuable, research has shown time and time again that people learn more and remember better when they enter into the process of discovery for themselves. In inductive study, commentaries, books, tapes, and other information about the Bible are consulted only after you have made your own thorough examination of the

Scriptures. These, then, can serve as a sounding board for your own observations and conclusions.

Actually, you may already be familiar with some of the principles of inductive study. For example, if you have ever taken any biology courses, you have studied frogs, and you have probably done so through observation.

To thoroughly study the frog, you first go to a river or creek bank where frogs live. You watch their eggs hatch and the tadpoles emerge. You see their back and front legs develop and grow, until they look like frogs and leave the water. After observing how the frogs respond to their new life on land, you catch one and observe it more closely. Eventually you take it to the biology lab where you dissect it to see how it looks on the inside. Afterward, you read what other biologists have learned about frogs to see if your conclusions match.

Inductive study of the Bible involves the same process: You begin with the Bible, observe it in its environment, and then take it apart so that you understand it firsthand. Then, when you've seen or discovered all you can on your own, you compare your observations with those of godly men and women who have written about the Word down through the ages.

Now, it would be much easier to just sit down and read a book about frogs in the first place and forget about traipsing through the marsh, wouldn't it? But you would end up with only secondhand knowledge.

You would know what others have said about frogs, which might be interesting and—you hope—true. But you never would have had a personal encounter with a frog.

Inductive Bible study draws you into personal interaction with the Scriptures and thus with the God of the Scriptures so that your beliefs are based on a prayerful understanding and legitimate interpretation of Scripture—truth that transforms you when you live by it.

If you will study inductively, the benefits will be beyond anything you have ever hoped could happen in your own personal understanding of the Word of God. As a result of incorporating the principles of inductive Bible study that we present in this book, you will

- be equipped to study God's Word on your own,

- be independent of relying only on another's interpretation,

- increase your knowledge of God and His ways,

- be greatly strengthened in your personal faith,

- recognize the authority of the inerrant Word of God in your daily walk, and

- become increasingly aware of all that it means to be in Christ.

Well, my friend, this little book is a good place to start. It is focused on the first of the three major components of inductive Bible study, which is **Observation**. But it is important to understand how they all work together.

Beginning with the Basics

Observation

Inductive Bible study consists of three component parts, which we will look at separately, but which frequently overlap in practice. These three parts are observation, interpretation, and application.

Observation answers the question: *What does the passage say?* It is the foundation which must be laid if you want to accurately interpret and properly apply God's Word. Have you ever read a book, chapter, or verse of the Bible and five minutes later been unable to remember anything you have read? So often we read the Bible with our eyes but not with our mind. There are several reasons for this. Either

- we think God's Word will magically make an impression on us without any effort on our part, or

- we don't really believe we can understand what we've read, or

- we are waiting for the pastor to teach on

this section of Scripture so we'll know what to believe.

Often, however, we forget what we have read simply because we don't know what to look for in the text. Therefore, in this book you are going to learn what to look for when you read your Bible.

Because observation is discovering what the passage is saying, it requires time and practice. You'll discover that the more you read and get to know a book of the Bible, the more its truths will become obvious to you. You'll be awed at the wealth of spiritual riches contained in even the shortest books of the Bible—and you will have discovered it yourself! You will know that you know!

Interpretation

Interpretation answers the question: *What does the passage mean?* And the basis for accurate interpretation is always careful observation. Interpretation is the process of discovering what the passage means. As you carefully observe Scripture, the meaning will become apparent. However, if you rush into interpretation without laying the vital foundation of accurate observation, your understanding will be colored by your presuppositions—what *you* think, what *you* feel, or what *other people* have said, rather than what God's Word says.

Interpretation is not necessarily a separate step from

observation, for often, as you carefully observe the text, at that very moment you begin to see what it means. Thus, interpretation flows out of observation.

However, interpretation can also involve separate actions or steps that go beyond merely observing the immediate text. One of these exercises is investigating cross-references. First and foremost, let Scripture interpret Scripture. You may also use other helps, such as word studies or the evaluation of resources such as commentaries and Bible dictionaries to check your conclusions or to supplement your understanding of the historical or cultural setting of the text.

Application

Application answers the question: *How does the meaning of this passage apply to me?* Usually this is the first thing we want to know when we read the Bible, but proper application actually begins with belief, which then results in being and doing. Once you know what a passage means, you are not only responsible for putting it into practice in your own life, but accountable if you don't! Ultimately, then, the goal of personal Bible study is a transformed life and a deep and abiding relationship with Jesus Christ.

Application is not a third step in the inductive process. Rather, application takes place as you are confronted with truth and decide to respond in obedience to that truth. The basis for application is 2 Timothy 3:16-17:

> All Scripture is inspired by God and prof-
> itable for teaching, for reproof, for cor-
> rection, for training in righteousness; so
> that the man of God may be adequate,
> equipped for every good work.

When you know what God says, what He means, and how to put His truths into practice, you will be equipped for every circumstance of life. To be equipped for every good work of life—totally prepared to handle every situation in a way that honors God—is not only possible, it is God's will. And that's what you will learn how to do if you will apply these study principles. Oh, the hundreds of stories we could tell you about what God has done because people disciplined themselves to know His Word in this way. It would thrill your heart! But right now, stories aren't our purpose; getting you into the Word inductively is! Then, friend, you can tell your own story! We'd love to hear it!

How Observation, Interpretation, and Application Relate to Each Other

Accurate interpretation and correct application rest on the accuracy of your observations. Therefore, it is vital that you develop observation skills, even if at first they seem time-consuming or you feel less than adequate and even awkward doing them. Studying inductively is a learning process that does not happen overnight. It happens by doing—doing over and over again, until the doing becomes almost a habit, and a wonderful one at that.

As you go through the inductive process, you'll sometimes find observation, interpretation, and application happening simultaneously. God can give you insight at any point in your study, so be sensitive to His leading. When words or passages make an impression on you, stop for a moment and meditate on what God has shown you. Bring the plumb line of truth against what you believe and how you are living.

When you know what God says, what He means, and how to put His truths into practice, you will be equipped for every circumstance of life.

Through a diligent study of God's Word, under the guidance of His Spirit, you'll drop a strong anchor that will hold in the storms of life. You will know your God. And when you know your God, not only will you be strong, but you will do great exploits for Him (Daniel 11:32).

1

The Rule of Context—
Context Rules!

Now, let's sit down and begin. And where do you begin? You begin by observing the text as a whole. By the text we mean whatever portion of Scripture you want to study. We suggest you study the Bible book by book, because each book of the Bible is a complete message in and of itself, that in turn relates in a special way to the whole Word of God. So choose your text—a book of the Bible—and then keep the following principles before you.

Step One:
Begin with Prayer

You are about to learn the most effective method of Bible study there is. Yet apart from the work of the Holy Spirit, that's all it will be—a method.

John 16:13-15 tells us that the One who guides us into all truth, the One who takes the things of God and reveals them to us, is the Holy Spirit, our resident

Teacher. So ask God, by His Spirit, to lead you into all truth and to open your eyes that you may behold wondrous things out of His Word (see Psalm 119:18 KJV). Begin with prayer—and continue with an attitude of prayer.

Step Two:
Identify the Context

Inductive study begins with a thorough evaluation of the context.

One of the most important principles of handling the Word properly and studying the Bible inductively is to interpret Scripture in the light of its context. Why? Because *context always rules in interpretation*.

The word *context* means "that which goes with the text." In general, then, context is the environment in which something dwells, the setting in which something exists or occurs. Remember the tadpole in the creek? Context is the creek!

In Bible study, context is the words, phrases, and sentences surrounding a particular word, phrase, or sentence. This context gives meaning to the particular word, phrase, or sentence and helps you understand what the author is saying. Context can also be expanded to paragraphs, chapters, books, and eventually the whole Bible. Because context rules in, or determines, the interpretation of the passage, it is important for you to know the context of any passage that you're studying.

To illustrate how context gives meaning to words, let's look at the word *trunk*. Suppose someone were to ask you, "What does the word *trunk* mean?" How would you respond? Well, if you were going to give a helpful as well as an accurate answer, you would first have to ask, "How is the word used?" because the word *trunk* can mean different things.

A trunk could mean the luggage compartment of a car, the flexible snout of an elephant, a large rigid piece of luggage used for transporting clothing and personal effects, the main stem of a tree, or shorts worn for swimming.

Therefore, the only way to know the intended meaning of the word *trunk* is to examine the context in which the word is used. The environment (the surrounding text) in which the word appears will show you which of these possible meanings is intended.

For instance, what would the word *trunk* mean in the following account from a trip to Africa?

> I remember seeing this huge trunk appear before the window of our car. We had been informed to always line up our car in the same direction in which the elephant was going, in case he charged at our vehicle. As we saw this trunk swinging back and forth and the elephant's face coming closer, we knew it was time to leave!

Since context is "that which surrounds or goes with the text," what information in this passage gives us a proper understanding of the word *trunk* as it is used here?

Well, we see that the word *elephant* appears twice, and the trunk is described as "huge" and "swinging back and forth." By examining the context, therefore, we discover the facts that surround the use of this word and can determine that in this particular passage the word *trunk* means "the flexible snout of an elephant."

In inductive study, context is determined or identified in the same way—by carefully observing what is repeated in the text and seeing how it all relates. If you observe what is said and pay attention to the repeated words, phrases, or ideas, you'll clearly see the context in any book, chapter, or passage that you're studying.

Context is determined or identified by thorough, careful observation of the text. Therefore…

Step Three:
Observe the Obvious

When you observe the text, *begin by looking for things that are obvious*—in other words, *things that are easy to see.*

Facts about people, places, and events always capture our attention; therefore, people, places, and events are easy to see. Since these kinds of facts are often repeated, this also makes them easy to see.

If you keep your focus on the obvious, you will

discover significant or repeated ideas; these will, in turn, show you the context of the book, chapter, passage, or verse you are studying.

For example, if you decide to put together a rectangular jigsaw puzzle, where do you start? Which pieces do you look for first? The four corners, of course! Why? Because they are obvious: There are only four of them, and they are easy to find because they have two straight sides.

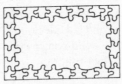

Once you identify the four corners, what do you look for next? Naturally, you look for the next most obvious things: the straight edges. Once again, they're the easiest pieces to find because each has one straight side!

By the time you have connected the straight edges, you have an outline or framework within which to put the other pieces together. You have established the context for the puzzle by looking for the obvious.

In a similar fashion, looking for the obvious facts, details, or ideas establishes the framework in studying a book, chapter, or passage of the Bible. So to put together a framework for the text, begin with the things that are obvious in that book.

As you observe the text and discover the context, however, you must always…

Step Four:
Deal with the Text Objectively

In other words, let the text speak for itself. Observing the text in order to establish context must be your primary objective, so let the text itself show you its repeated emphasis.

So often I fear our only reason for being in the Word is subjective—we simply want to get something for ourselves. To look for something that "ministers to our heart"—or to find a verse we can use to help someone or set someone straight.

How grievous this must be to God, who wants us to truly know Him and to be sanctified (set apart) by truth—and His Word is truth (John 17:17). Therefore, our primary goal—our driving passion—should be to know truth and then adjust our beliefs and our lives accordingly.

Now granted, certain portions of any book you are studying might minister to you more than other portions, but the truth and context never change. The message of the book itself will always be the same. It is truth—absolutes on which you can stake your life, your character, and your lifestyle.

So first, look at the Word objectively.

Yes, God's Word will minister to you personally. It will! It's a living Word. But to discover the context, you must first look at the text objectively to discover the repeated emphasis of the author. Then, when you personalize the Word, you'll know you are applying it correctly. And that's imperative.

Now as I say this, I must also caution you not to fail to look at Scripture subjectively as well. When you pause to reflect on what God is saying and how it applies to you, that is when God the Holy Spirit quickens His Word to your heart; that is when you know He has a message especially for you at a specific point in your life.

At the same time that you study the Bible inductively, read it devotionally. By devotionally I mean with a heart that wants to hear what God is saying to you. God speaks to us personally through His Word. Therefore, as you read and as you study, don't fail to take time to listen to your God.

Step Five:
Read with a Purpose

Reading with a purpose is accomplished by asking questions of the text. You must interrogate the text as a detective would a witness.

To get the whole story—all the details—journalists

are taught to ask the "5 W's and an H" (*who, what, when, where, why,* and *how*) in their reporting.

If you are going to read the Bible with purpose—to get all the details—you must ask the 5 W's and an H. Therefore, as you read, ask…

Who wrote it? *Who* said it? *Who* are the major characters? *Who* are the people mentioned? To *whom* is the author speaking? About *whom* is he speaking?

What are the main events? *What* are the major ideas? *What* are the major teachings? *What* are these people like? *What* does he talk about the most? *What* is his purpose in saying that?

When was it written? *When* did this event take place? *When* will it happen? *When* did he say it? *When* did he do it?

Where was this done? *Where* was this said? *Where* will it happen?

Why was there a need for this to be written? *Why* was this mentioned? *Why* was so much or so little space devoted to this particular event or teaching? *Why* was this reference mentioned? *Why* should they do such and such?

How is it done? *How* did it happen? *How* is this truth illustrated?

When you ask the 5 W's and an H of the text, and when you let the text provide the answers, you'll be amazed at what you learn. These questions are the building blocks of precise observation which, remember, lay a solid foundation for accurate interpretation.

Many times Scripture is simply misinterpreted because the context isn't carefully observed. Accurate answers from the text to the 5 W's and an H kinds of questions will help assure correct interpretation.

Let me illustrate this by simply using one verse:

"After these things Jesus was walking in Galilee; for He was unwilling to walk in Judea because the Jews were seeking to kill Him" (John 7:1).

As we interrogate the text with the 5 W's and an H, we discover that…

"Jesus" answers the question, *"Who* is this about?"

"Was walking" answers the question, *"What* was He doing?"

"In Galilee, not Judea" answers the question, *"Where* was He walking?"

"Because the Jews were seeking to kill Him" tells us, *"Why* was He not in Judea?"

"After these things" tells us, *"When* was this action taking place?"

"What things?" The things that took place in the previous verses.

That is how you use the questioning technique of the 5 W's and an H. And the more you do it, the more it will become a habit, until asking these questions becomes second nature to you as you study God's awesome book.

Now—and this is important—don't think you have to find all 5 W's and an H every time you question a passage, because they're not always going to be there.

For example, the verse above, John 7:1, did not answer an "H" question.

Simply read the text and answer all the 5 W's and an H questions you can.

Remember, every part of the entire process of inductive Bible study is based on asking who, what, when, where, why, and how kinds of questions. This is how vital the 5 W's and an H are!

Now, my friend, that you know the principles behind observation, let's move on to the process of observing the text. As you begin to do this, you're going to be excited by what you learn. And you'll probably find yourself saying, "I can't believe what I've seen all by myself!"

2

Getting the Big Picture

Although the Bible is a collection of 66 books written by many authors under the inspiration of the Holy Spirit, it was written one book at a time. And each book of the Bible has its own unique purpose and message.

If you've read much of the Bible, you know that many of the books cover similar material. Yet each book has its own place, value, and purpose in the whole counsel of God. So if you want to know your God intimately—to understand His mind, heart, ways, and how He wants you to live—you need to begin studying His Word book by book—one book at a time.

But with 66 books, where do you begin?

If you are new to the inductive study process, we suggest you begin with a short book.

Once you've chosen a book, your first step is to determine the type of literature. Follow the steps on the following pages, taking into account the type of literature.

Step One:
Begin on Your Knees

Prayer is crucial to Bible study. Since truth must be revealed by the Spirit of God, it follows that prayer must be an integral part of Bible study as you continually seek God's wisdom, counsel, and revelation. Give yourself time for the Holy Spirit to speak to your heart.

Step Two:
Read and Reread the Book

The more you read the book you have chosen to study, the more familiar you will become with it. There is no substitute for reading and prayerfully meditating on the Word of God. If you are studying a longer book, it may take several days to read the whole book through one time. But do it!

Your goal is to handle God's Word accurately. To do that, you've got to see the corners and find the straight edges, the boundaries. That is why it is easier to learn the inductive process with a shorter book.

The first time you read through the book, it may seem like a collection of verses that are barely related to one another. The more you read, however, the more you will see that all of those "isolated verses" really do belong together. Or when you read, you may come across some things which really puzzle you. Don't stop to try to figure them out. Now is not the time. Remember, first you look for the corners and straight pieces, then these difficult pieces will fall into place more easily.

As you read the book you are going to study, you'll also want to consciously…

Step Three:
Identify the Type of Literature

The type of literature determines the way you will handle the text. For instance, Hebrew poetry (such as the Psalms) is different from the historical books (such as Kings and Chronicles), and the historical books are different from the epistles (such as 1 and 2 Timothy), both in style and content. History books give background and tell of real events and how God dealt with real people, but you don't build doctrine on historical events. Most of the doctrine for the church is contained in the epistles. So, recognizing the type of literature you're studying is important.

As you read through the book, determine which of the following best describes the book you're studying.

Is It **Historical**?

The book of Genesis sets forth the history of God's creation from the beginning of time, while the book of Judges records the period of Israel's history when the judges ruled. The book of Acts tells the history of the spread of the gospel and the beginning of the church.

Is It **Biographical**?

The book of Luke gives a chronological biography of our Lord Jesus Christ from His genealogy through His resurrection.

Is It **Poetic***?*

The book of Psalms is Hebrew poetry.

Is It **Proverbial***?*

The book of Proverbs, considered wisdom literature, is a compilation of concise sayings which set forth wisdom and instruction. Proverbs are not to be interpreted as prophecies or doctrines.

Is It **Prophetic***?*

The book of Revelation describes itself as a book of prophecy. It tells of future events which are sure to come about.

Is It an **Epistle** *(Letter)?*

The book of 2 Timothy is a letter written to an individual. The book of Colossians is also a letter, but it is written to a church. The epistles contain most of the doctrine (teaching) for the church.

Is It a **Combination***?*

Some books can be a combination of different types of literature. For example, the book of Daniel is both historical and prophetic. It tells of past events but also predicts future events.

Now, once you determine the type of literature, you need to...

Step Four:
Deal with the Text Objectively

We mentioned this before, but it bears repeating, so listen carefully—be objective! Do not approach the Word of God subjectively, just to get something for yourself. Rather, come to the Word objectively, so God can teach you what you need to know. *Once you objectively see what God is saying, you'll know how that truth relates to you subjectively.*

Remember that context is identified by observing what is repeated over and over by the author. So in doing the overview of the book, you need to let the text speak for itself.

Step Five:
Use the 5 W's and an H

Be sure that you are reading with a purpose by interrogating the text with the 5 W's and an H. We covered this in the previous chapter, so you may want to turn back to that section and refresh your memory.

Step Six:
Discover Facts About People and Events

To discover the context of the book, begin by identifying the obvious. Depending on the type of literature you're studying, people and events are usually the most obvious and the easiest to identify.

Principle 1: Identify the Obvious Names

If, for example, you are studying one of Paul's epistles, you will first need to read through the book while looking for and identifying the facts about the author, the recipients of the epistle, and any other people who are mentioned. If you're studying a different type of literature, such as one of the historical books, you will initially look for any mention of people in general as well as the specific events covered in the historical account. In prophetic literature the author may or may not be prominent, but people and events will be.

So keep all this in mind and, according to the type of literature, adapt what we're teaching you about seeing and identifying the obvious.

As you identify the facts about people and events, you begin to discern the historical and cultural context in which the author is writing. And this, of course, reflects on what he writes and how he writes.

Although God is the ultimate author of Scripture, He specifically chose certain human beings to write down His truths for Him (2 Timothy 3:16; 2 Peter 1:20-21). The books of the Bible are like light that comes through a prism. The prism separates the light, bringing out different colors and hues, yet it is still from one source—light. Therefore, many books of the Bible are also an expression of the human author: his background, his experiences, and his philosophy of life. Although the Bible is timeless, and every word divinely inspired, each book was written during a certain time period; therefore, each book is colored by the historical setting in which it was written. The political, social, philosophical, and even religious conditions of the times all came to bear on what was expressed on paper, yet without distorting or detracting from what God wanted written down for us.

To fully understand a book, all of these factors must be considered. This can be done by simply asking the who, what, when, where, why, and how kinds of questions about the people and events mentioned in the book.

You may have thought that the only way to understand the occasion and historical setting of a book was to read books about the Bible. But now you know that careful observation of the Word of God itself will reveal these facts to you. Isn't that exciting?

Now then, here are some practical steps to follow in order to identify the obvious.

STEP 1: If you're studying an epistle, read through the text and mark in a distinctive way every mention of the author, the recipients, and other people. As you do, look for facts about each person—facts that are unique to his or her identity and circumstances.

If you're studying history, watch for the main characters in each of the events. Marking every pronoun is not necessary, but this is a matter of personal preference. In prophecy, the message is more central, although Old Testament prophecy sometimes includes historical references to people who figure prominently in historical books.

In a distinctive way, mark every mention of each person or group of people, as well as the pronouns (such as *I, me, my, we, us, our, who, whom, you, they,* and *their*) that refer to them.

Scripture can be marked distinctively in one of three ways:

- by coloring each use of the same word and its synonyms in one color or a combination of colors

- by drawing a diagram around that particular word to distinguish it from others*

- by combining color with a diagram. For instance, you could color *repent* yellow and then draw a diagram with it.

Whichever method you use, be consistent. Mark the text in this same manner throughout all the chapters of the book you are studying.

STEP 2: As you mark the references, ask 5 W's and an H questions like the ones below. Some items apply only to the letters, such as author, recipient, and reason for writing.

---

* Be careful in your use of diagrams, as too many of them can become distracting when reading your Bible. I prefer to use colors and color combinations when possible and limit my diagrams. Colors enable me to spot the recurrence of words easily and quickly.

Who is the author?

Who are the recipients?

Who is this person?

What does he tell you about himself?

What are his circumstances?

Where is he? Record any references to geographical locations. Also, turn to a map and locate these places. (*The New Inductive Study Bible* has maps right in the text.)

Why is he there? These questions will give you clues to the historical setting of the book. Then ask...

Why is he writing? *Why* are they doing this? *Why* is this being said to them?

As you ask these kinds of *Why* questions, the purpose of the book will become obvious. If the author doesn't give you a specific reason for writing, then the purpose will be revealed in other ways as you get more detailed in your observations.

Purpose usually only applies to letters. The purpose for historical books is to communicate the content that you might learn about God and His ways. The purpose of prophetic books is to communicate the message, usually relating to judgment, and to learn about God and His ways. Wisdom literature varies from book to book, but again, the message is the key feature.

- Ask, *What* does the author talk about the most? *What* are the people to do or not do?

As you ask these questions, the repeated emphasis in the book will show you the theme of the book. For all books except the letters, the book theme is usually more easily developed after all the chapter themes have been determined. Occasionally, such as in the Gospel of John, the text gives a clear statement.

STEP 3: This step is only for letters: Make a list of all you learn about the author and the people mentioned. This list will come from what you learned by marking the references and asking the 5 W's and an H and will give you valuable insights that will help you interpret the text properly.

Principle 2: Identify the Obvious Events

Are any events mentioned in the book? Remember, people and events are always the easiest to see; in fact, events may be more obvious than people. Therefore, as you read through the book, notice what events, if any, are mentioned in each chapter.

Once again, the type of literature, the purpose of the book, and the structure of the book can all be determining factors in what is the easiest to see.

For example, in the first 11 chapters of the book of Genesis, the focus is on four main events. Although people are mentioned, the events are the most obvious. Therefore, if you were studying this book, you would make a list of the event(s) described in each of these chapters.

The repetition of certain words and phrases shows that the emphasis in Genesis 1 is on the event of *God's creation of the world*. In Genesis 3 the primary events are *the temptation of Eve by the serpent* and *man's choice to disobey God*. In Genesis 6–10 the event is *the flood*.

Marking the text and listing the facts surrounding these four main events will clearly show the emphasis in each of these first 11 chapters.

However, in Genesis 12–50 the emphasis switches from events to people—in fact, four major people: *Abraham, Isaac, Jacob,* and *Joseph*. Therefore, you would mark the text and list the facts about these people, which would clearly show the primary emphasis in each chapter. Then, you'd look at the events of their lives and examine them in the light of the 5 W's and an H. Ask...

> *What* is happening?
>
> *Where* is it happening and *When*?
>
> *Who* is involved?
>
> *What* are the consequences of this event?

This process may appear laborious as you simply read through these instructions; however, once you actually put it into practice, you'll see how profitable it is.

But what do you do if the mention of people or events gives no real insight into the message of the book? For example, in the epistle of James the references to people and events do not really help you discover the context of the book. So where do you go next? You go to the next obvious thing: You look to see what subjects or topics the book deals with.

Step Seven:
Mark Key Words

As you read and reread the text, you'll begin to notice that certain key words and/or phrases are repeated throughout the book, in a certain segment, or in several segments of the book.

Key words are words that are vital to understanding the meaning of the text. Like a key, they "unlock" the meaning of the text. A key word might be a noun, a descriptive word, or an action word that plays a part in conveying the author's message.

A key word or phrase is one which, when removed, leaves the passage devoid of meaning.

Often key words and phrases are repeated in order to convey the author's point or purpose for writing. They may be repeated throughout a chapter, a segment of a book, or the book as a whole.

For example, in the book of 1 John the words *love, sin, abide,* and *know* are repeated throughout the book, whereas *fellowship* is repeated only in chapter 1.

You'll want to mark each key word, along with

synonyms and pronouns, in a distinctive way or color. A synonym is another word that means the same thing in the context being considered. A synonym is another way of saying the same thing.

For example, in the book of 2 Timothy, note these synonyms for *suffering*:

> chains (1:16)
>
> hardship (2:3,9)
>
> persecutions (3:11)

The value of a distinctive marking system cannot be overestimated. Whichever way you choose to mark key words and their synonyms, mark each key word the same way every time you observe it throughout your study of the Word. Then, in future study, you will be able to track key subjects and quickly identify significant truths throughout Scripture.

If you want to be consistent, list key words, symbols, and color codes on an index card and use it as a bookmark in your Bible. Be sure to mark pronouns (*I, you, he, she, it, we, our, who, whom, which*) and synonyms (words that have the same meaning in the context) the same way you mark the words to which they refer.

Key phrases and statements also give important repeated emphasis and/or show organization in a book.

For example, in the book of Judges the repetition of the statements "the sons of Israel again did evil," "there was no king in Israel, and... [man] did what was right in his own eyes" is key to understanding the message in Judges.

In the book of Haggai the phrase "the word of the LORD came [to]... Haggai" helps unlock the structure and purpose of the book.

It is imperative that you observe key words and phrases because they reveal the author's intended message, his intended emphasis, and how he will accomplish his purpose.

Every key word is a *Who* word or a *What* word or a *When* word or a *Where* word or a *Why* word or a *How* word. Therefore, every key word will answer one of these questions: *Who? What? When? Where? Why?* or *How?*

KEY WORDS

▼

SUBJECTS

▼

THEME

Key words reveal the subjects. Subjects reveal the theme.

The more a word is repeated, the more obvious it becomes that the word represents a subject. The more that subject is repeated, the more obvious it becomes that the subject represents a theme in the book.

Step Eight:
Discern the Main Theme of the Book

Now that you've worked through the previous instructions, see if you can discern the statement that best summarizes the book (the summary statement). As we mentioned earlier, for all books except the letters, the book theme is usually more easily developed after all the chapter themes have been determined. Occasionally, such as in the Gospel of John, the text gives a clear statement. If you're not studying a letter, make this your last step.

As you do this, let the book reveal the theme to you. You do not have to "come up with" a book theme. It should be obvious. But if it's not, don't subjectively create a theme in your mind, based on emotion or *your* favorite passage. Discerning the main theme or summary statement should be an outgrowth of an objective evaluation of the repeated emphasis in the book. That is why, my friend, you need to give adequate time to the overview of the book.

The shorter the book, the easier it will be to discern the theme. So you may want to wait until you finish your At a Glance chart (see step 9) before you try to discern the theme.

Once you discern the theme (whenever that is—no rush!), look for a verse in the book that best covers or expresses that theme. That verse will become your key verse for the book.

Finally, write out a summary statement of the book.

The very process of doing this will help crystallize the theme of the book, as well as seal it in your mind—and heart. Then, in the future, you'll know what book of the Bible you need to turn to in order to meet a specific need for truth or insight.

As you write out the theme, use as many key words from the text as possible and be as concise as you can. For example, in the Gospel of John the words *believe* and *life* are repeated over and over throughout the book. Then, at the end of the book, John clearly states his purpose:

> Therefore many other signs Jesus also performed in the presence of the disciples, which are not written in this book; but these have been written so that you may believe that Jesus is the Christ, the Son of God; and that believing you may have life in His name (20:30-31).

So, the key verse would be John 20:30-31. The summary statement for the Gospel of John should center on the author's purpose: Written that you might believe that Jesus Christ is the Son of God; and believing have life in His name.

To look at another example: In the book of Hebrews the repeated emphasis is that Jesus is our great High Priest, so that could adequately serve as a summary statement for the book. The key verses could be Hebrews 4:14-16.

Step Nine:
Develop an At a Glance Chart

An At a Glance chart is such a helpful tool for future reference, as well as giving you a quick synopsis of the book. Constructing such a chart will give you an invaluable visual overview of the book, which will enable you to see how the parts (the chapters) relate to the whole (book), which in turn will help you analyze the structure of the book you are studying.

If you have *The New Inductive Study Bible*, you'll find an At a Glance chart at the end of each book of the Bible. If not, you can create your own by using the example we've provided. After you fill it in, you'll always have that information with you. And you'll always be able to find where various truths are dealt with in the book. In long books this is an indispensable tool, for in a matter of seconds you can skim through the overall content of the book.

Step Ten:
Discover the Theme of Each Chapter

Do this the same way you came up with your book theme (see step 8).

A chapter theme should fall within two parameters: First, is it the main subject dealt with in that chapter? And second, does the theme relate to the overall book theme? If your choice of a theme or summary statement is truly the theme of the chapter, it will clearly relate to the book theme.

EPHESIANS AT A GLANCE

Theme of Ephesians:

SEGMENT DIVISIONS

		CHAPTER THEMES

Author:

Date:

Purpose:

Key Words:

every reference
to being in
Christ
(in the Lord)

according to

the (Holy) Spirit

rich(es)

in the heavenly
places

once (at one
time)

grace

power

body (church)

redemption
(acquire)

walk

the devil
(including
powers, rulers,
authorities, etc.)

		1
		2
		3
		4
		5
		6

Once you have the theme, record it on the At a Glance chart in the appropriate column. Do this for each chapter of the book.

Eventually, as you study the book chapter by chapter, you will choose a key verse for each chapter that reflects or provides the basis for what you have chosen as the chapter theme.

Step Eleven:
Identify Clearly Defined Segments

A segment division is a major division in a book, such as a group of verses or chapters that deal with the same subject, doctrine, person, place, or event.

Now, just as you don't subjectively create chapter themes, you don't subjectively create segment divisions. Rather, you discover them from the text. The context of the book determines the segment.

Not every book has clearly defined segments. However, if the book does divide into segments, you'll find that the number and type of divisions will vary according to the type of literature you are studying and according to the size of the book. A book might be divided (segmented) according to

- dates
- places
- topics
- doctrines

- reigns of kings
- major characters
- major events

For instance, the book of Romans divides into two segments: chapters 1–11 are doctrinal; chapters 12–16 are practical.

In the book of Genesis, chapters 1–11 focus on four major events, and chapters 12–50 on four major characters.

In the book of Revelation, the divisions are clearly stated in Revelation 1:19: "Therefore write the things which you have seen, and the things which are, and the things which will take place after these things."

The segment divisions are: "the things which you have seen" (chapter 1); the "things which are" (chapters 2 and 3); and the "things which will take place after these things" (chapters 4–22).

Discerning segment divisions requires time, practice, and a familiarity with the content of the book and the context in which it's laid out. Usually you will discover even more possible divisions after you have studied the book for a while. Therefore, the segment division part of your At a Glance chart will be developed more completely as you become more familiar with a book.

Well, my friend, this is how you do an overview of a book. It's the most crucial part of all inductive study, for it sets the context for correctly interpreting and applying the text.

Now then, in the next section we'll take you step-by-step through the process of observing a book a chapter at a time. When we do, you will be excited about what you learn.

By the way, I'm so proud of you for making this effort to see truth for yourself. You will never regret it. God is going to open a whole new world of understanding to you…and you are going to be so grateful to Him.

3

Focusing In on the Details

Once you've done your overview, you're off to a good start. Now you're ready to study the book chapter by chapter.

To go back to the illustration we used in the previous chapter, you've finished surveying the property from the air. Now it's time to start surveying the land on foot, looking at the details. Or to return to our frog illustration, it's time to get the frog out of the pond!

In the overview, you discovered the basic framework of the book. Now your goal is to focus in on the more detailed observations of the content of each chapter.

Remember, the overview process is usually best only for letters. The previous chapter's instructions work perfectly for each chapter of the Bible book you are studying. The steps in this chapter are designed for letters. However, the various devices in steps 5 and 6 are helpful.

Step One:
Remember to Pray

As you start observing the book one chapter at a time, remember truth is revealed by the Spirit, so begin with prayer and continue in prayer. Luke 24:45 says, "Then He [Jesus] opened their minds to understand the Scriptures."

Step Two:
Keep the Context in Mind

Don't forget that each chapter, and each truth contained in that chapter, must be considered in the context of the whole book, so remember all you learned in the overview. Keep it before you. It's foundational.

Step Three:
Does the Text Answer Any of the 5 W's and an H?

Although the following may be a little repetitious, bear with me. Repetition and review are an integral part of the learning process. I will be brief, but let me emphasize this once again: Develop a questioning mindset. Remember to keep asking the 5 W's and an H as you read the text. Although the text may not necessarily have the answers to each question, it will still help you observe exactly what is being said. Ask questions such as...

Who spoke it? About *Whom*? *Who* are the major characters? *Who* are the people mentioned? To *Whom* is the author speaking?

What are the main events? *What* are the major ideas?

What are the major teachings? *What* does the author talk about the most? *What* is his purpose in saying that?

When did this event take place? *When* will it happen? *When* did he say it?

Where was this done? *Where* was this said? *Where* will it happen?

Why was there a need for this to be written? *Why* was this mentioned? *Why* was it not mentioned?

Why was so much or so little space devoted to this particular event or teaching? *Why* was this reference mentioned?

How is it done? *How* is this truth illustrated?

Accurate answers from the text to these kinds of questions will help assure correct interpretation.

As you read, look only at the things that are obvious. If you focus on the obvious, ultimately those things that are obscure will become clearer.

Also, as you read, questions of interpretation will come to mind. When these questions arise, write them on another sheet of paper. Do not attempt to answer these questions until you have thoroughly observed the text.

Step Four:
Look for and Mark Key Words and Phrases

Remember, a key word is a word the author uses repeatedly in a significant way, or a word which cannot be removed from the text without leaving it devoid of meaning. A key word might be a noun, a descriptive word, or an action word that plays a vital part in conveying the author's message.

You have already marked some key words during the overview. Now, continue the process on the same Observation Worksheet, building upon what you discovered in the overview. "Walking through the text" at a slower pace, you will see other key words and phrases that you didn't notice before.

As with the overview, when you discover more key words and phrases, you will want to mark them in a distinctive way on your Observation Worksheet. You can do this either by coloring each use of the same word and its synonyms and pronouns in one color or by drawing a distinctive diagram around that particular word to distinguish it from others. Remember, colors are preferable. Eight-color Pentel pencils or Crayola Twistables are available for this purpose at most Christian bookstores. They are sold in conjunction with *The New Inductive Study Bible*.

You are now looking for words that are key to this particular chapter, even though they may not be key in any other chapter.

Every key word is a *who, what, when, where, why,* or *how* word.

At this stage, mark only one key word at a time as you read through the chapter. This means every time you mark a different key word, you'll read through the chapter again. Thus, if you are marking five key words, you will read the chapter five times.

Marking the text in this way helps you slow down and soak in the content of the chapter, letting the Holy Spirit minister truth to you as you read and reread the Word. As a matter of fact, when you read Scripture over and over again you will find yourself automatically remembering it. You will also find yourself beginning to hide God's Word in your heart, rather than just skimming along making colorful marks on paper. The important thing is not the marking, but what you learn by marking that word.

All references to God the Father, the Son, or the Holy Spirit should be considered key words. Depending on how frequently they occur in the text, you may or may not want to mark them. You may simply want to make a mental note of them. Whichever way you choose, as you mark or note references to the Father, Son, and Spirit, ask the 5 W's and an H kinds of questions regarding the text. For instance…

Who is this—God, Jesus, or the Holy Spirit?

What is this telling me about God, Jesus, or the Holy Spirit?

Why is this mentioned?

Be careful that you don't just go through this marking process by rote, mindlessly marking the words. Be sure that you are really reading the text and thinking about it so that you comprehend all it has to teach you about God, Jesus, and the Holy Spirit.

The value of marking and evaluating the references to God, Jesus, and the Holy Spirit is that you begin to build a firm foundation in your understanding of the Trinity—understanding the differences between the person and work of God, Jesus, and the Holy Spirit as the Bible defines them and understanding the similarities.

Step Five:
List What You Learned About Each Word

A list is a compilation of every fact given about a particular word, subject, person, place, or event in a single chapter. These facts are answers to the 5 W's and an H.

Put each list on a separate sheet of paper, heading it with the key word. (After you have refined your lists, you can transfer them to the margin of your Bible or worksheet.) For example, if you made a list on *God* from 2 Timothy 1, it would look something like this:

When you evaluate this list, you will notice that the subject of salvation has come up (2 Timothy tells us that God saved us, God called us, etc.). With this, you have the basis for another list, which brings us to an important principle: As you observe the text, you're going to stumble onto topical lists, such as this one on the subject of salvation.

Salvation
1. God saved us (v. 9)
2. God called us with a holy calling (v. 9)
   – not according to our works (v. 9)
   – according to His purpose and grace (v. 9)
3. was granted to us in Christ Jesus (v. 9)
   – from all eternity (v. 9)
4. now has been revealed by the appearing
   of our Savior Christ Jesus (v. 10)

Be on the alert for topical lists. As you can see from the list on salvation, remember that not all lists of truths are formed from key words. However, key words are usually the basis for a list.

Step Six:
Look for Contrasts, Comparisons, Terms of Conclusion, and Expressions of Time

Contrasting Words and Phrases

A contrast is an evaluation of things that are different or opposite in the context being viewed. Many times, contrast is noted by the word *but*.

For example, note the contrast between what God has and hasn't given us in 2 Timothy 1:7:

"For God has not given us a spirit of timidity, but of power and love and discipline."

However, as you look for contrasts, remember the contrast is not necessarily between the actual words. It can be a contrast within the thought or body of truth conveyed by the words in that particular context.

For example, the words *night* and *day* seem like an obvious contrast. Yet in the following context, they are not. In 2 Timothy 1:3 Paul says:

"I constantly remember you in my prayers night and day."

This is not a contrast, but shows that Paul prays during both times.

However, in 1 Thessalonians 5:5 he uses *night* and *day* to contrast the sons of light and the sons of darkness:

"For you are all sons of light and sons of day. We are not of night nor of darkness."

Therefore, make sure that you are not just marking contrasting words, but contrasting thoughts.

Many times the words *but, however,* or *nevertheless* show a contrast. When you see those words, read the context to see if two different things are being compared.

You can make a mental note of the contrast, or if you prefer, you can note the contrast in the margin of your Bible or right in the text like this:

> 1:7 For God has not given us a spirit of
> timidity, but of power and love and
> discipline.

What truth is being revealed through the contrast? What point is the author making through the contrast? That's what you want to discern.

Words of Comparison

A comparison always refers to things that are similar or alike. Many times the words *like* and *as* signify a comparison.

Determine, if possible, what truth is being revealed through the comparison. Then note the comparison in the margin or mark it in the text. For example in 2 Timothy:

> 2:3 Suffer hardship with me, as a good soldier
> of Christ Jesus.

Expressions of Time

Words such as *then*, *after this*, *until*, and *when* show timing or sequence of events. They answer the question *When?*

Make a note in the text of any reference to time. As you mark these expressions of time, observe what you learn from noting "when" something occurs, which can be crucial when it comes to interpreting the text. This is especially seen in passages like Matthew 24:15-31, where the "whens" and "thens" lay out the sequence of events.

Expressions of time can be marked by drawing a clock in the margin or by simply drawing a clock face over the word itself. Personally, I also color my clock green so I can spot it even more easily.

Terms of Conclusion and Result

Words such as *therefore*, *for*, *so that*, and *for this reason* indicate that a conclusion or summary is being made or that a result is being stated. Therefore, watch for such terms!

You may want to underline these as you observe them in the text. Here is an example from 2 Timothy:

> 1:7 For God has not given us a spirit of
> timidity, but of power and love and
> discipline.
>
> 1:8 Therefore do not be ashamed of the

testimony of our Lord or of me His
prisoner, but join with me in suffering for the gospel according to the
power of God.

The conclusion? Because God has given us a spirit
of power, love, and discipline—rather than timidity—
we are not to be ashamed of the testimony of our Lord.

Other terms of conclusion or result in this chapter are:

1:4 longing to see you…so that I may be
filled with joy.

1:6 for this reason I remind you…(What
reason? Verse 5 tells us: "because of
the sincere faith within you.")

1:12 For this reason I also suffer these
things…(What reason? Verse 11 says:
because "I was appointed a preacher
and an apostle and a teacher.")

This, friend, is how to watch for contrasts, com-
parisons, expressions of time, and terms of conclusion
or result.

Step Seven:
With Historical or Biographical Books

If you are studying historical or biographical books,
it is helpful to record the following:

- The location and/or timing of the opening of the chapter. You can put this information just above the first verse on your Observation Worksheet, if you're using one, or in the margin of your Bible.

- Any significant changes in location or time as they occur in the chapter.

- Major characters, doctrines, and events covered in the chapter. Record this information at the end of your Observation Worksheet or on a sheet of paper under each category.

Major Characters   Major Doctrines   Major Events

These summations will not only help you in the future, but will serve to help you observe and analyze exactly what is in that chapter.

Step Eight:
Check Chapter Theme

Now that you've come this far, simply check out the chapter theme you determined when you did your overview. Does it adequately describe the main teaching of the chapter? If so, congratulate yourself. If not, change it—then congratulate yourself for seeing your need to make the change.

Step Nine:
Develop Memorable Paragraph Themes

Some people like to do paragraph themes or write out statements that summarize the content of each paragraph in the chapter. Although this means more work on your part, the very process of doing this will give you an even better grasp of the text.

Just as the book theme is supported by and carried out by the chapter themes in the overview, here the chapter theme is supported by and carried out by the paragraph themes.

From the Whole to the Parts

Remember that *at every point you have gone from the whole to the parts.* You began by looking at the whole book, getting an overview of the book, discovering its theme. Then you moved to its parts, the chapters, discovering the chapter themes.

Now you are moving from the whole chapter to its parts, the paragraphs and their themes.

The paragraph divisions in your Bible are shown by an indentation at the start of a paragraph, or the paragraph symbol, or boldface type for the verse number of the first verse of the paragraph, or some combination of these. Check to see what method your Bible publisher has used.

What can make doing paragraph themes somewhat difficult is that the chapter and paragraph divisions are man-made. They even differ from translation to translation.

Although there might be differences in paragraph divisions, however, it doesn't change the author's original flow of thought.

Let the Paragraph Talk

If you do paragraph themes, use the same rules you used for the book and chapter themes. Just remember, you do not ever have to "come up with" a paragraph theme or summary statement. All you have to do is let the paragraph reveal the theme to you, and then analyze the contents of the paragraph to discover the best summary statement.

Evaluate the truths in the paragraph and, using words from the text, summarize the content of the paragraph in as few words as possible.

Your theme needs to be descriptive of the paragraph's theme and yet distinctive from the other chapter or paragraph themes.

Choose the paragraph themes in light of the chapter theme.

When you do paragraph themes, it is best to write them in the left margin of your Observation Worksheet opposite the paragraph.

Often in an epistle, the first paragraph will just be a salutation to the book.

For example, a possible way to describe the first

paragraph in 2 Timothy 1 would be "From Paul to Timothy" or "To Timothy."

The following outline shows you the flow of thought all the way from the book theme to the paragraph theme.

> Book—theme
>> Chapter 1—theme
>>> Paragraph 1—theme
>>>
>>> Paragraph 2—theme
>>>
>>> Paragraph 3—theme
>>
>> Chapter 2—theme
>>> Paragraph 1—theme
>>>
>>> Paragraph 2—theme
>>
>> Chapter 3—theme
>>> Paragraph 1—theme
>>>
>>> Paragraph 2—theme
>>>
>>> Paragraph 3—theme
>>>
>>> Paragraph 4—theme

If you carry out this process throughout the book you are studying, you will have a comprehensive outline of the book comprised of the main themes of the paragraphs and chapters of the book.

When you do the overview, you will have more

questions than answers, since you are only getting the big picture. As you do a more detailed chapter study, you will find many of those answers.

However, even if you haven't, keep your list before you. Resist the temptation to go to your commentaries until you've done some more personal work with the text. That's what we'll look at next.

Are you concerned, my friend, that you are not going to come up with the right answers? Relax; don't panic. These are skills that are developed through repeated use until they become second nature. You do the best you can, and God will meet you there. He knows your heart and will honor your diligence. Remember, those who succeed are those who determine to keep on keeping on until they learn. I always tell my students, "Hangeth, thou, in there!"

The Next Step

Hopefully this little book has given you the tools you need to be more effective in observing the biblical text. But in a sense, we are just getting started. We've looked at some tools that will help you read more carefully and get more out of every Scripture passage you read. Now, if you want to continue to develop your Bible study skills, you'll want to get a copy of our book, *How to Study Your Bible*, by Kay Arthur, David Arthur, and Pete De Lacy. This book will teach you the critical skills you need so that after you have carefully *observed* the text, you can properly *interpret* and *apply* it to your life. There is also a helpful workbook available that lets you put what you have learned into practice as you study specific biblical passages.

Finally, if you enjoy this method of study, you'll want to get a copy of *The New Inductive Study Bible*, which contains all the fill-in-the-blank charts you'll need for your studies, as well as maps, background information, and more.

Welcome to the world of inductive study! May God richly bless your study of His Word!

About the Authors

Kay Arthur is a four-time Gold Medallion award-winning author, member of NRB Hall of Fame, and beloved international Bible teacher. She and her husband, Jack, cofounded Precept Ministries International to teach people how to discover truth through inductive study. Precept provides teaching and training through study books, TV and radio programs, the Internet, and conferences in over 180 countries and 70 languages.

David Arthur, chief executive officer of Precept Ministries International, came to Precept after serving as vice president of Generous Giving, where he directed communications and publications. He also served several years as a pastor in the Presbyterian Church of America and Associated Reformed Presbyterian denominations. David has contributed to several Precept publications and teaches on "Precept Upon Precept" videos.

Pete De Lacy, executive vice president of published products for Precept Ministries International, is also the author of many studies in the New Inductive Study Series and a contributor to *The New Inductive Study Bible* and *Discover the Bible for Yourself*. Pete is also a featured teacher on many "Precept Upon Precept" videos.

NOW AVAILABLE IN
NASB® & ESV®

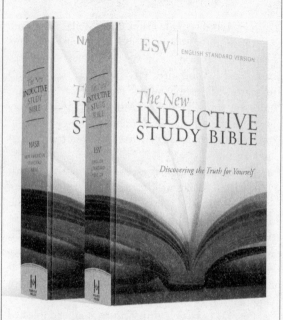

The Gold-Medallion-winning *New Inductive Study Bible* (more than 700,000 sold) is now available in the trusted English Standard Version as well as the New American Standard Bible version. This Bible is based entirely on the inductive study approach, leading readers directly back to the source and allowing God's Word to become its own commentary.